LITT
BASIC

by Dan Zevin

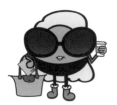

Illustrated by Dylan Klymenko

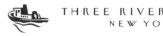

THREE RIVERS PRESS
NEW YORK

Little Miss Basic lived in a basic McMansion with her basic mommy, Mrs. MILF; her basic daddy, Dr. Midlife Crisis; and her basic hypoallergenic, nonshedding Labradoodle, Beyoncé.

Family

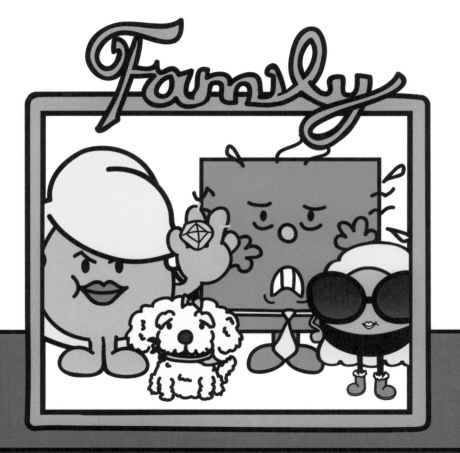

One day, she got dumped by her boyfriend, Mr. Douchebag.

●●●○○ AT&T
1:52AM
50%
Messages
<3 bae
Contact
its over. sry lol
lol ur so ridic <3
srsly were done
wtf ??!?!! what about apple picking? what about our tix 4 bey's concert!!
omggggg ur literally the worst right now
</3

She was so super depressed she, like, *literally* beat herself up over it.

KEEP CALM AND BE BASIC
IVE
LAUGH
LOVE

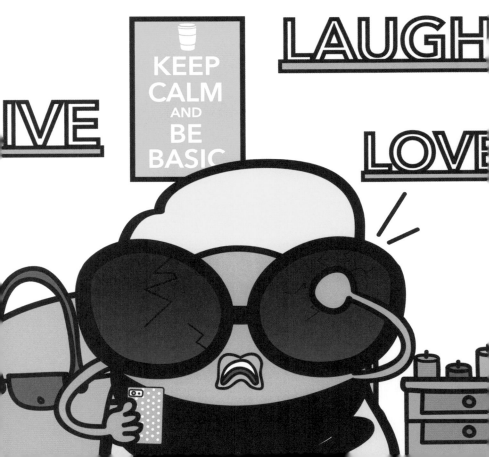

Then she cried all night into her big Coach purse.

Worst. Day. Evs.

The next morning, Little Miss Basic reached out to her bestie, Little Miss Baysic.

"He said I'm not his type," Little Miss Basic confided to Little Miss Baysic.

"OMG, you're not *any* type," Miss Baysic reassured Miss Basic. "You are exactly the same as everyone else!"

CALM
AND
BE
BASIC
CALM
AND
BE
BASIC

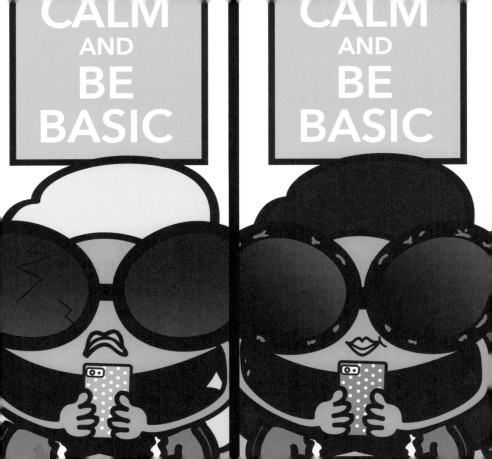

Well, that was totes the sweetest compliment literally anyone in history could have given her.

She was speechless!

It was her first time ever.

Miss Basic searched and searched for just the right words to express her profound gratitude to Miss Baysic.

":)," she declared.

And then they met at Starbucks for pumpkin spice lattes.

BASIC

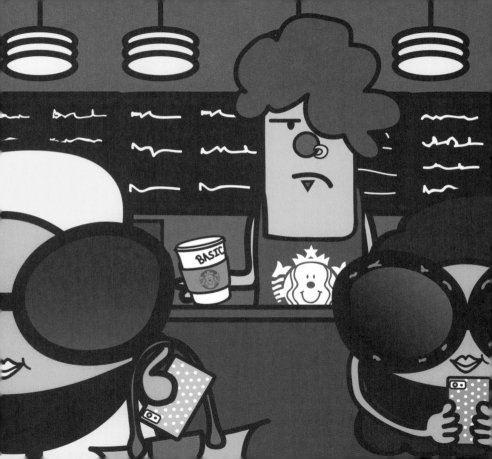

One day, Little Miss Basic's Instagram status said:
UGH.

Can you guess what photo she posted?

Her UGGS!

And can I just say?
They were literally?
A million years old?
Because Little Miss Basic?
Wore them literally?
24/7?

Instagram
lilmissbasic
12m
770 likes
lilmissbasic UGH #iwokeuplikethis #blessed #icant
view all 25 comments
lolwut so ratchet
omgeewhiz literally

She wore them for mannies *and* peddies.

She wore them for SoulCycle, rebounding, and Pilates.

She wore them with her black North Face jacket, her black Lululemons, and her black Kate Spade spectacles.

She even wore them for premarital relations with Mr. Douchebag!

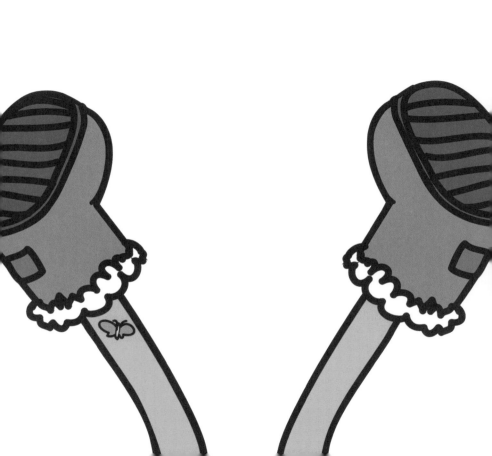

One sunshiney Sunday, Little Miss Basic drove her Jetta to the big city for brunch.

She was so super excited, she literally texted everyone in the world until she got there.

It would be her very first meal since she started her juice cleanse!

~my fave~
sry lol
omg yasss!!!
literally?!!

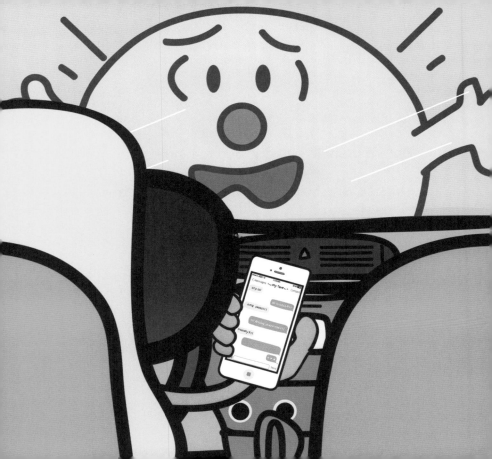

Before brunch, she decided to binge on fro-yo.

Outside, she spotted a man relaxing on the sidewalk.

"He is doing Savasana pose," Miss Basic observed.

"But, *ew*! His yoga mat is ratchet!"

19 HANDLES

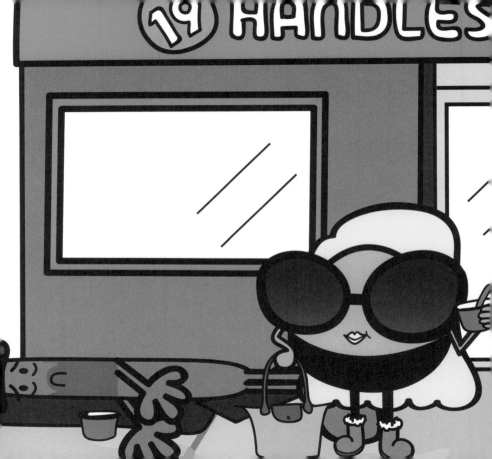

Still, she couldn't help but admire what a skinny betch he was.

He is vegan, she thought. *Or possibly paleo.*

Just then, the yogi greeted her in a friendly way.

He was like, "My name is Mr. Homeless and my tummy is hungry."

"I know, right?" Miss Basic said sympathetically. "When I'm cleansing? I'm literally so starving? I can't even."

19 HANDLES

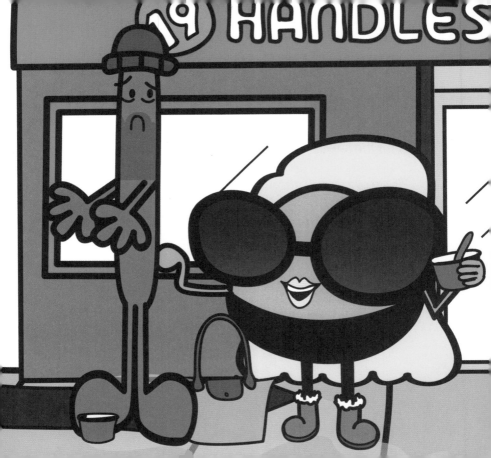

Mr. Homeless had never met a Basic before.

There was so much he wanted to ask her.

"Do you have any money for food?" he curiously inquired.

"Shut. *Up!* Are you, like, *psychic*?!" exclaimed Little Miss Basic. "I was just about to expense my Sunday brunch!"

AMX
1234 5678 4100
L.M. BASIC
BASIC BITCHES PUBLICITY INC

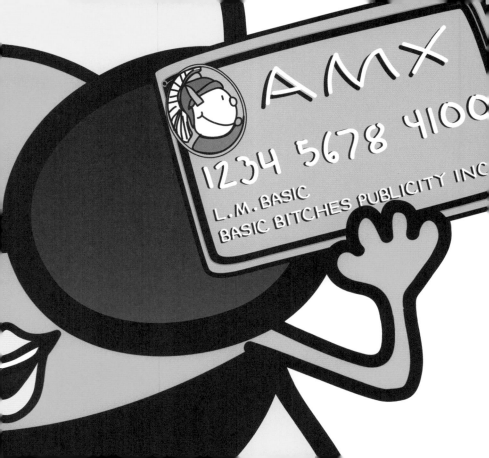

And together they went off to get gluten-free pancakes and mimosas.

THREE RIVERS PRESS and the Tugboat design are registered trademarks of
Penguin Random House LLC.

Library of Congress Cataloging-in-Publication Data is available upon request.

ISBN 978-1-101-90444-2
eBook ISBN 978-1-101-90456-5

PRINTED IN CHINA

Illustrations by Dylan Klymenko
Cover design by Dylan Klymenko

10 9 8 7 6 5 4 3 2 1

First Edition